IMPROVING PEER RELATIONSHIPS
Achieving Results Informally

Norman C. Hill

A FIFTY-MINUTE™ SERIES BOOK

CRISP PUBLICATIONS, INC.
Menlo Park, California

IMPROVING PEER RELATIONSHIPS
Achieving Results Informally

Norman C. Hill

CREDITS
Managing Editor: **Kathleen Barcos**
Editor: **Carol Henry**
Typesetting: **ExecuStaff**
Cover Design: **Carol Harris**
Artwork: **Ralph Mapson**

Copyright © 1996 by Crisp Publications, Inc.

Printed in the United States of America by Bawden Printing Company.

Distribution to the U.S. Trade:

National Book Network, Inc.
4720 Boston Way
Lanham, MD 20706
1-800-462-6420

Library of Congress Catalog Card Number 96-83625
Hill, Norman C.
Improving Peer Relationships
ISBN 1-56052-305-0

This book is printed on recyclable paper with soy ink.

LEARNING OBJECTIVES FOR:

IMPROVING PEER RELATIONSHIPS

The objectives for *Improving Peer Relationships* are listed below. They have been developed to guide you, the reader, to the core issues covered in this book.

Objectives

☐ 1) **To explain the need for attention to organizational peer relationships**

☐ 2) **To discuss techniques of good peer relationships**

☐ 3) **To point out problems in peer relationships**

Assessing Your Progress

In addition to the Learning Objectives, *Improving Peer Relationships* includes a unique new **assessment tool*** which can be found at the back of this book. A twenty-five item, multiple choice/true-false questionnaire allows the reader to evaluate his or her comprehension of the subject matter covered. An answer sheet, with a chart matching the questions to the listed objectives, is also provided.

* Assessments should not be used in any selection process.

ABOUT THE AUTHOR

Norman Hill is the Continuous Learning Team Leader for Houston Lighting and Power Company where he is responsible for organization improvement, training and career planning, and management development activities. He has previously worked for Exxon Co., USA as a Human Resources Manager and National Training and Development Services, Inc. as a consultant. He has published widely on leadership, personal development, and organization improvement activities including five previous books and more than 25 articles in business-related journals. An earlier book, *Increasing Managerial Effectiveness* received the best book in management award for 1980 from Learning Resources International. He has conducted workshops and seminars in the United States, Europe, and Central America. In 1992, he was selected as a Leadership Fellow by the Kellogg Foundation. He has a Masters Degree in Organization Behavior from the Marriot School of Management at Brigham Young University.

ABOUT THE SERIES

With over 200 titles in print, the acclaimed Crisp 50-Minute™ series presents self-paced learning at its easiest and best. These comprehensive self-study books for business or personal use are filled with exercises, activities, assessments, and case studies that capture your interest and increase your understanding.

Other Crisp products, based on the 50-Minute books, are available in a variety of learning style formats for both individual and group study, including audio, video, CD-ROM, and computer-based training.

CONTENTS

P A R T

I

What Are Peer Relationships?

WHAT ARE PEER RELATIONSHIPS?

In an organization, people work together to get things done. To achieve results, the organization coordinates activities *formally*, through supervision, policies and rules, as well as *informally*, through meetings, networking and shared projects. In a restaurant, for instance, the manager who develops policies about how cooks and servers should work together is using *vertical* coordination. When the servers and cooks talk directly to one another, they are coordinating *laterally*. It is the *peer relationship* that facilitates this lateral coordination.

The ultimate success of the restaurant is built on its reputation. This reputation can suffer even through the restaurant produces culinary masterpieces. The host or maître d' must be friendly and efficient. Servers must present the food at the correct temperature, and get the check to the table without too much delay. Table attendants need to keep water glasses filled and empty plates removed to make way for new courses. The wine steward needs to serve the requested vintage at an appropriate temperature at the correct time. The efforts of all these peer groups must smoothly mesh. An enjoyable meal depends as much on how well a restaurant coordinates its multiple activities as on the excellence of the food it serves. Food quality also requires tight coordination among the various actors in the kitchen. When the actions of one group or individual in an enterprise depend significantly on those of others in the enterprise, coordination becomes crucial to the success of that enterprise.

Vertical coordination occurs when people at higher levels manage and control the work of subordinates. Lateral coordination is more informal. It occurs when those at similar levels—peer groups—respond to one another face-to-face.

What are some examples of lateral coordination in your organization?

_____

_____

_____

What are some examples of lateral coordination breakdowns in your organization?

_____

_____

THE IMPORTANCE OF PEER RELATIONSHIPS

In any organization, people perform specialized tasks. As an organization becomes larger, the need increases to divide work into separate activities. Because one person "can't do it all," others become involved and the work gets divided up. But as soon as this division of labor occurs, it's necessary to figure out how best to assemble it all into the final product.

Sometimes people in an organization aren't aware of the effort it takes both to divide up work adequately and put it back together efficiently. They assume that "if everybody does what they are supposed to do," there will be no need to manage interfaces or to cultivate peer relationships. They may even label difficult peer interfaces as simply "office politics." These assumptions are wrong. Except where jobs are extraordinarily simple, it takes time and skill and an understanding of the dimensions of peer relationships to make an organization work. Information, resources, and influence travel laterally in an organization as well as vertically in the hierarchy. It requires skill and knowledge for a manager to be effective in both lateral and hierarchical interactions.

To ensure that tasks are meshed, duplication is avoided, all parts add up to the whole and work objectives are met, an organization needs communication and coordination. This might mean that people have to check with their peers to be certain, for example, that a particular vendor is the "best" from an overall company point of view and that the negotiated terms of an agreement don't make it difficult for others in the organization to get their own "good" contract terms. No matter how an organization or company is organized—by product, service, function, region or customer—important information and coordination requirements outside the work group will require its members to work with others who are neither subordinates nor bosses.

Chart Your Peer Relationships

In the space below complete the lateral organization chart of you and your peers. Write your name in the center circle and the names of peers in the boxes. Add more lines and boxes if needed.

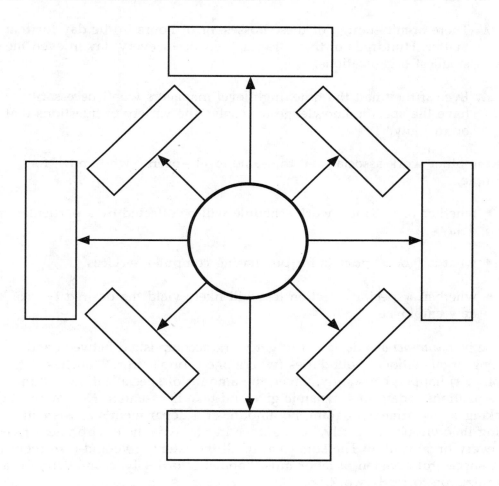

With how many peers do you interact? _____

Had you paid much attention before now to how many peers you actually interact with? _____

Did you find you had to add extra boxes? _____

Does your peer group extend to other departments? _____

THE IMPORTANCE OF PEER RELATIONSHIPS (continued)

All the lateral coordination that goes on in every organization can't be handled with just advance planning or written procedures alone. Nor is it always the answer to refer to some high-level boss who has a broad enough perspective to make a wise, organization-wide decision. There are two reasons for this.

1. There aren't enough of these bosses, or of hours in the day for that matter. Hundreds of these transactions occur every day in even the smallest organizations.

2. Even if they had the time, high-level managers won't necessarily have the specific knowledge to resolve the variety of questions that occur daily.

It's the other work associates at the same level—peers—who know, for example,

- whether or not their work schedule will be affected by a particular delay

- what a "good" price is for purchasing computer services

- whether a specific selection test will likely yield the desired type of new employee

These *peer transactions* designed to get work accomplished between and among organizational boundaries (where one group's "turf" touches another's) happen constantly. Given the amount of specialization within organizations today, this dynamic give-and-take is essential. No amount of sticking to a planned program, no amount of a department's consistently doing its own job "correctly," can suffice in the dynamic environment faced by every organization. The sum total of all the lateral give-and-take required in a successful division of labor must happen effortlessly, seamlessly, for an organization to really work.

COMMUNICATION: THE CRITICAL FACTOR

Communication breathes the first spark of life into an organization, and communication keeps every organization alive. Nothing else is so crucial to coordination of effort. No other factor plays such a precious role in building and preserving trust among people.

> **Communication is the make-or-break issue.**

It's not enough for the right hand to know what the left hand is doing. The right hand needs to know what the left *intends* to do. People need a keen sense of what's planned if they are to execute with precision. There's not much hope of orchestrating a coordinated effort unless good communication precedes action.

Jammed-up information pipelines and warped messages can cause conflict and cripple a group's performance. When people settle for second-rate communication, they sabotage high-quality work by leaving it up to somebody else. Talking about the need to "better communicate" occurs all the time. But talk is cheap. Face reality.

What stops you from communicating better with others in your organization?

_____

_____

_____

_____

COMMUNICATION: THE CRITICAL FACTOR (continued)

Everybody in a work group needs to know what's going on. The information network should link all the players, connecting everyone on the team. People in an organization must meet . . . talk . . . engage—and do it with a lot of give-and-take. People need to be encouraged to air their differences, to go public with their opinions. That's the only way to achieve understanding, work out the best approach, and end up with everybody agreeing on a solution.

Anybody who is left out—who gets information too late or not at all—can interrupt coordination and cause disaster. Everyone can be a quality control point in the communication process, can help make sure that data is accurate, up-to-date, and meaningful. Anyone who makes a move based on mis-information can wreck the group's results.

THE THIRTEENTH FAIRY

"And when eleven of them had bestowed their gifts, in came the uninvited thirteenth fairy, burning with revenge for having not been invited to the Princess's christening feast, and, without greeting or respect, she cried in a loud voice, 'In the fifteenth year of her age the Princess shall prick herself with a spindle and fall down dead.'"

From *Sleeping Beauty*

Who has not had a "thirteenth fairy" show up at just the wrong moment? Perhaps one has made an untimely appearance at the end of a planning session, or maybe one has made a home somewhere in a production line. The "curse" brought by such people is in the form of resistance to change, or even sabotage. Examples can be found in many real-life situations—not just in fairy tales.

In your organization, how often in the process of planning or while introducing change into a system does the thirteenth fairy, having been omitted from the initial planning, show up in the middle of things to curse the entire effort?

_____

_____

Thinking of a specific example, what was the result?

_____

_____

This issue of including the "right people" is of special significance. Managers are continually faced with the task of deciding whom to include (or, better yet, whom not to exclude) in meetings that will bring about change. The work done by researchers in communications relative to *opinion leaders*—people whose choices affect the choices of others—is particularly relevant when we are appointing the participants in ground-floor change activities. This research constitutes a good point of departure, and we'll look at it more closely.

THE THIRTEENTH FAIRY (continued)

> ## *Opinion Leaders*
>
> **"Must we not then first of all ask whether there is any one of us who has knowledge of that about which we are deliberating? If there is, let us take his advice, though he be only one, and not mind the rest; if there is not let us seek further counsel."**
>
> **—Plato**

Elihu Katz and Paul F. Lazarsfeld were among the first to single out *opinion leaders*. Katz and Lazarsfeld defined a two-step flow of communication (mass media to opinion leader to mass audience) that has rapidly gained a following. The opinion leader was, and still is, esteemed for his or her ability to act as a source of information and of social pressure toward a choice, and a social support to enforce the choice once it has been made. Sell the opinion leader, and he or she will in turn sell your product.

Opinion leaders exist in virtually all primary groups. Some are actual group leaders in authority, others are innovators who occupy no assigned position of leadership. Whether they are group leaders or merely influencers, and regardless of their area of interest, opinion leaders usually have several characteristics in common. The effective opinion leader

- Does not differ greatly from his or her peers in attitudes, political values, mannerisms, personal experience or occupational prestige

- Is usually well acquainted with the attitudes of the group

- Expresses an opinion frequently, at least in his or her own field of influence

- Makes judgments and expresses them while others are still undecided

- Is generally more talented in verbal skills and interpersonal communication than his or her peers

One popular generalization is that the opinion leader is more likely than his or her peers to attend professional fairs, conventions, and meetings. This leader reads more professional journals, newspapers, magazines and printed material, and acquires more information from radio, television and lectures. In short, the opinion leader has greater contact with outside sources of information than do other members of the group.

There are certain people you just should not leave out when it comes to making organizational changes. Regardless of what you call these people, an awareness of these individuals is a must for the prudent manager. If excluded, such persons can become a thirteenth fairy.

Think of a project or activity that did not get approved or, if approved, was unsupported by others. Was the "thirteenth fairy" syndrome at work? What were the consequences? Who was "left out"? In retrospect, how might opinion leaders have been included at key events?

_____

_____

_____

_____

_____

_____

Sometimes the answer is just deciding to be responsible for improving things—even if it's "not your job." When something is portrayed as everybody's responsibility, it will likely end up as nobody's responsibility. Describe an example in your work group now where it seems that a work process has problems because all responsibilities are not clearly defined.

_____

_____

_____

_____

_____

_____

THE THIRTEENTH FAIRY (continued)

Everybody, Somebody, Anybody and Nobody

This is a story about four people, Everybody, Somebody, Anybody and Nobody. An important job needed to be done, and Everybody was asked to do it. Everybody was sure Somebody would do it. Anybody could have done it, but Nobody did it. Somebody got angry about that because it was Everybody's job. Everybody thought Anybody could do it, but Nobody realized that Everybody thought Anybody could do it, and Nobody realized that Everybody wouldn't do it. It ended up that Everybody blamed Somebody when actually Nobody asked Anybody.

FORMING PEER RELATIONSHIPS

Peer relationships require effective *partnering* for easy give-and-take to occur. Partnering is found in any endeavor that requires the effort and talents of more than one person, such as a sports team, an orchestra, or the design group for a supercomputer. People also band together as a way of coping with stress. Study groups formed to help students get through the first year of law school, for instance, create a bond that continues long after graduation. Medical doctors who survive their internship together experience a very strong camaraderie. In these situations, group members cooperate for mutually reinforcing reasons:

1. Your feeling of goodwill toward the group

2. Your belief that survival is more likely if you collectively share and watch out for one another

Emergencies: The Formation of Powerful Bonds

Sometimes "turf issues" develop in an organization and make it difficult for strong peer relationships to develop. But certain conditions can transcend these organizational barriers. One of the most dramatic examples of a strong peer network occurs among law enforcement officers and emergency rescue personnel. Investigating a criminal incident, saving flood victims and fighting forest fires require intense planning and demand strong informal peer networks. Although rivalries do occur and may inhibit peer relationships, the urgency of a life-threatening situation can overcome these hindrances. This kind of camaraderie is seldom duplicated in less dramatic, everyday situations. An FBI agent once noted, "If I trust another officer or even a volunteer with my life, then trusting him or her with anything else seems like a minor matter. And once having extended my trust so completely, I naturally want to do anything else I can for them, share any information with them, make their life as easy as possible."

FORMING PEER RELATIONSHIPS
(continued)

Because such compelling peer relationships develop naturally in life-threatening and emergency situations, they provide some useful insights into how work settings can better incorporate the same conditions. In emergencies, we care very little about others' race, personality, political views or economic status. Instead, we recognize intuitively that "there is a job to be done," and we accept someone's good intentions at face value. The other person is there to help get things done, to respond to the crisis as quickly and efficiently as possible. More often than not, peers within an organization have the same intentions, but they are not automatically understood or accepted. But emergencies focus our attention very efficiently. We know that we are "all in this together."

For those trained to respond to them, emergencies are a time for action and mutual dependence on others. Those in charge must rely on whomever is available. No one is wasted, and time must be used well. Emergency and law enforcement personnel come to rely on one another as if their lives depend on it—because they do. It is the network that counts. One person acting alone, even if they are "doing the right thing," can actually inhibit a rescue operation. Individual capabilities matter less than mutual action.

Instinctively, faced with danger or a crisis, emergency personnel act together to accomplish their mission. They reach out to anyone available or willing to help, sharing knowledge and resources to get the job done. And in the process, they form a common bond that lasts beyond the emergency event. Having endured some hardship together, they have a bond that can last a long time.

Strong peer networks that transcend organizational barriers and interpersonal competition can also be forged in more ordinary environments. Sometimes it happens when people work together for a good cause. Early in the twentieth century, Jane Addams, Julia Lathrop and Florence Kelley formed the inner circle of Hull House, an organization dedicated to women's issues of the day. Unlike their disciples and apprentices, Addams, Lathrop and Kelley were comrades-in-arms. They addressed each other in their letters as "Dear Sister" and developed a sense of unity and dedication to an ideal based on respect, commitment and love.

▽? *What conditions in a group or organization promote this type of peer interaction?*

_____

_____

_____

_____

_____

_____

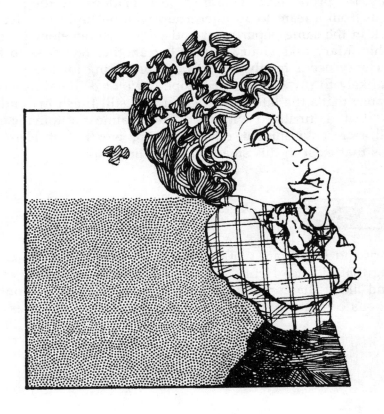

WHY PEER RELATIONSHIPS CAN BE DIFFICULT TO MAINTAIN

Peer relationships can develop strains and stresses even under the best of conditions, because they are affected by the behavior of the people involved. Interaction among peers and demands on their time are unpredictable.

To many people, spending a majority of their time coordinating with others suggests that the organization is somehow misshaped, that someone is not a team player. But there are more logical reasons why most lateral work relationships present a difficult challenge. Leonard R. Sayles has described seven conditions that make peer relations more difficult simply because people work in different departments or groups and thus have specialized needs in getting things done.

1. Intragroup versus Intergroup Contacts

Essentially, the problems of lateral or peer relations are the problems of adjustment from a team to an intergroup relationship. Consider two people who work in the same department and who have developed a close working relationship. Mary asks Henry to give her another few days to finish the analysis Henry needs for the report he is preparing for top management. Henry is likely to say, "Sure, but I hope it won't be delayed any longer than that, because that's the latest I can get it and still finish my end on time." And the "deal" is finalized with that simple, almost automatic, exchange. In this small, team environment, other problems won't exist. Here are four conditions that exist in this small team relationship:

Shared Values

Since Mary and Henry are working closely together, Mary won't ask for something that violates Henry's professional norms or group values. She knows and likely shares these values with him. She will ask only for modifications consistent with the standards, norms, and values they share.

Established Image and Precedent

Henry won't be concerned that his concession will place him in a lower status role in the future, which might encourage more special treatment or interference with the routines necessary for efficiency.

Common Interests

Henry won't be anxious about whether Mary's demand was simply a tactic to delay completion (e.g., because the report will injure her interests) and to gain some strategic advantage to the detriment of Henry's section. Again, they share strategic goals; they are not competitive.

Interpersonal Understanding

Mary won't use mannerisms or approaches that antagonize Henry. They have learned to interact in order to minimize stress for both of them. Repeated exchanges like this one have perfected their give-and-take skills.

After a great deal of interaction and long experience with give-and-take that allow for fitting both their personalities and jobs together, Henry and Mary are able to work through differences without creating tension. Most peer relations, however, do not have the luxury of frequent interaction that produces such shared values, interests and understanding. Further, most intergroup working relationships generate demands that involve competing interest simply because there aren't as many shared goals.

We might experience some team relationships that are as simple and automatic as the relationship between Henry and Mary, but the nature of work itself typically inhibits such relationships.

WHY PEER RELATIONSHIPS CAN BE DIFFICULT TO MAINTAIN (continued)

2. Irregularity of Contact

At any level of the organization, as long as individuals are interacting regularly, they will typically evolve easy methods of transacting their business. Except for the occasional personality conflict, members of organizations learn to adopt comfortable routines of give-and-take to exchange ideas and help as they work together. The comfortable perfection of this cooperation reaches its zenith in settings like the hospital operating room or on the athletic playing field. Hardly a full sentence is spoken, yet coordination exists; just a glance, a muttered word, or a wink communicates all another person needs to know to adjust their behavior to yours. It is only when people are irregular in their contacts that they must explain and expound—often in lengthy and discomforting detail. One could almost say "Words are for strangers; body language is for colleagues."

3. Interference with Routines and Subgoals

Not only is there an unanticipated quality about these intergroup contacts, but they also represent a threat in most cases. As "work" crosses departmental boundaries, inevitable differences in values will affect what is done, how and when. Say a clinic sending patients to a centralized test/analysis facility is seeking to routinize its own work, and certain tests can best be done in lots, with the equipment adjusted to settings for each lot, or at special times of the day. It's easy to understand why there will be differences to resolve over issues such as the flow of patients moving from clinic to testing.

The classic controversies between development staff and manufacturing staff are numerous. Development engineers conceive the new project in terms consistent with their own professional standards, perhaps involving important technical breakthroughs and complexities worthy of a major product innovation. The manufacturing managers, on the other hand, are sensitive to the difficulty of translating sophisticated concepts into low-cost, routine, quality-controlled production. Naturally, there will be enthusiastic exchanges, as each department doubts the other's willingness to cooperate.

4. Lack of Equilibrium in the Organization

Many of us do not appreciate that in organizations, small problems can cause major dislocations. The reason is not difficult to understand: Organizational equilibrium is frequently disturbed because of the many interrelationships made necessary by technical dependencies. Many people have tasks that depend directly on the performance of other tasks. On paper it looks as though no contact is necessary, and indeed it isn't—as long as everything works perfectly. But the minute something unplanned occurs and requires approval and consensus, there is a domino effect, and the equilibrium is damaged.

5. Repeated Contacts Are Required

Most projects require analysis, discussion and stops and starts simply because difficult issues are not easily resolved. Looking for answers to real organizational issues can be compared to panning for gold in a stream. After considerable effort we may finally see something shiny at the bottom of the creek and pull it out to examine it more closely, only to discover that its the "wrong rock". This process of looking, sifting, and finding the "wrong rock" occurs frequently in panning for gold and in working on challenging projects and tough assignments in organizations. Repeated contacts with others who have vital information—but other work priorities of their own—may be required simply because its not possible to tell what's real gold and what's simply a shiny rock until it is closely examined. Unfortunately, this repeated contact can come across to others as wasted motion or not thinking things through enough the first time. It is, in fact, simply all part of the discovery process. It requires time and patience and mutual support to make these interrelationships work smoothly so that the right information is used in the sifting process.

Each concession creates issues and problems for other departments. People must go back again and again to see others who control access or releases. Almost every action requires extra effort for all concerned—more seeking of information, more persuasion of others to change their procedures, more replanning and more rescheduling. Each full circle of contacts brings some new concessions and yet more problems to be worked through.

WHY PEER RELATIONSHIPS CAN BE DIFFICULT TO MAINTAIN (continued)

6. Ambiguities Abound

Only occasionally does anyone have much doubt about who is asking for what with a request. This is not true of many of the lateral peer relationships we are talking about.

EXAMPLE: *Getting Specific*

A Plastics department calls on the Research and Development division for some help with the design of a new product. Somewhere, sometime, upper management has decreed that R and D should help the Plastics Division in its efforts to produce commercially viable products. But how much help, at what "price," and with what time priority have been left unspecified. Similarly, it will make a substantial difference to R and D if Plastics defines the problem very narrowly and wants a highly specific technical answer—involving a kind of testing service—or if they want high-level professional counsel on a much more general problem. R and D wants challenging, general problems, but it's likely that Plastics wants specific service work.

Further, both because of as yet undefined needs and because the future status of an executive or department depends on the relationships that emerge from these negotiations, they are made even more difficult. In other words, Plastics and R and D are concerned with more than just identifying a specific request for assistance. Interpretation of the request may well affect the relationship of R and D to many other parts of the organization, as well. It's not difficult to predict that R and D is worried about becoming a pure service activity, always handling the needs of other departments and unable to shape broad, professional standards and concepts for itself.

As long as services and products have to be priced, subject to various management and economic formulas, there will be inevitable ambiguities in numbers that all interests will want to try to exploit. Finance wants a price that will shorten the payback period for the new investment; engineering may want to seek a higher price to justify unanticipated development costs; and marketing, aware of other competition, suggests a lower price.

Negotiation and Persuasion

Because of the ambiguity of both the Plastics request and the R and D mission, the people of both departments will learn they must devote a lot of time to peer relationships. Not only are there lots of these relationships, but they seem to require selling, persuasion and influencing—distinct from the simpler giving and receiving orders.

7. Steady Stream of New Roles

Most organizations are constantly introducing new functional requirements—for instance, a specialist to cope with the growing consumer movement—without taking into account the consequences on others' jobs.

Consider the predicament of Ann Smith, appointed as a Consumer Specialist. What is her job? She's told that she is responsible for assisting the corporation in interpreting and responding to consumer knowledge, consumer complaints and the growing sensitivities of the customer.

► Does Ann proceed to evaluate and criticize what divisions and managers are doing?

► Can she stop production if she becomes aware that potentially serious product safety and liability questions exist about one of the company's products?

► With whom does she collaborate and how?

► How does she get information, criticism and assistance into the hands of operating managers?

These and other issues result from ongoing changes in an organization's staff.

WHY PEER RELATIONSHIPS CAN BE DIFFICULT TO MAINTAIN (continued)

To summarize, peer relations pose distinctive challenges because such relationships have the following characteristics:

✓ They involve intergroup relationships.

✓ They are irregular.

✓ They interfere with routines.

✓ The number of contacts is so great.

✓ They multiply in quantity because of unstable conditions and the need for concessions and repetition.

✓ The required relationship is often ambiguous.

✓ Management keeps adding new specialists.

Take a few minutes to analyze your own peer relationships at work.

Where are things going well? Where are the "pinch points"? How can you change what you do to address these seven conditions inherent in any peer relationship?

_____

_____

_____

_____

_____

_____

PART

II

Developing Positive
Peer Relationships

GUIDING PRINCIPLES

Everyone gets battered about occasionally in an organization. But letting it keep us from goal achievement and day-to-day work satisfaction is to get robbed twice. Don't allow broken trust and unmet expectations, though painful, to deprive you of the energy you need to achieve your goal, nor of the satisfaction you get from a job well done.

When things go wrong, it is not just a matter of your "rights" being violated. When you belong to a community or organization, you have certain responsibilities. A major one is to contribute to making things better for everyone, not just yourself. But when you stay physically while withdrawing emotionally, you take up resources that someone else might better use.

As organizations become more complex, their technologies more sophisticated and their environments more turbulent, the need for effective peer interaction increases. To meet that need, organizations may form task forces to be used when new problems arise or opportunities occur that demand the resources of various organizational people, specialties or functions. Extensive use can be made of coordinating roles and units, that is, individuals and groups whose sole purpose is to help their peers work together effectively and integrate their efforts.

EXERCISE: Attitude Check-up

	Yes	No
1. I am not present at work emotionally.	☐	☐
2. I no longer work or contribute with enthusiasm.	☐	☐
3. I work with someone who is withdrawn emotionally.	☐	☐
4. I feel that I have unmet expectations at work.	☐	☐
5. I feel unmotivated and don't really care what is going on.	☐	☐

If you answer yes to even one of these questions, this section will be especially useful for helping you re-examine your work attitudes.

GUIDING PRINCIPLES (continued)

> ## CASE STUDY: Ellen
>
> Ellen is a product manager responsible for the introduction of new soap products. She works with several departments, including Market Research, the developmental laboratory, Production, and Sales. In designing the new product, Market Research usually conducts a test of consumer reactions. Hank, the Market Research head, wants to run the standard field test on the new brand in two preselected cities. Ellen is opposed to this because it would delay the product introduction date of September 1. If she can meet that date, Sales has promised to obtain a major chain-store customer whose existing contract for another brand of this type of soap is about to expire. On the other hand, Manufacturing is resisting a commitment to fill this large order by the September 1 date because new-product introductions have to be carefully meshed into their schedule with other products the facilities are producing.

What are Ellen's major challenges?

_____

_____

_____

Author's Comment

Ellen's complex job is to negotiate with Market Research and Manufacturing. This means assessing the importance of their technical criteria, determining which conditions are modifiable and deciding what is best for the new product's introduction overall. Her goal is to balance the legitimate objections of Manufacturing and Sales as she perceives them against her own need to get the new product off to a flying start.

MATRIX STRUCTURES

Many organizations move to *matrix structures* that formally spell out both vertical and lateral coordinating responsibilities.

Permanent Matrix Structure

These contain two sets of managers, with relatively equal power and somewhat opposed interests, who are supposed to negotiate their differences. The systems managers are the store- or regional-level executives, responsible for operating a diversified department store that is responsive to the consumer tastes of particular communities and areas. They are dependent for their merchandise on equivalent functional managers—divisional merchandise managers. The latter identify, specify, and purchase the major categories of merchandise the stores will carry—furniture, for example, or tires or women's fashion apparel. These two sets of managers have separate performance responsibilities, report up separate lines of authority, and see the world from separate perspectives—the former from a store in a particular place or geographical area, the latter from the perspective of the overall market.

Shifting Matrix Structures

These draw members from functional departments. Formal and informal meetings provide structural opportunities for dialog and decisions but can absorb an excessive amount of a manager's or employee's time. Task forces offer a source of integration around a specific problem but can detract attention from ongoing operating issues. Liaison roles or groups can effectively span different positions or divisions but are heavily dependent on the skills and credibility of those who carry out the boundary-spanning activities.

At least three questions occur persistently for people in their efforts to develop positive peer relationships at work:

1. What is really happening in this relationship?

2. Why do others act as they do?

3. What can I do about it?

MATRIX STRUCTURES (continued)

Here are some suggestions for addressing these issues:

► **Emphasize Common Goals and Mutual Influence in Relationships**

Even in difficult relationships, there are likely to be shared goals. Both parties want to be effective managers. Neither is likely to benefit from a fight to the finish. At times, each party needs the help or collaboration of the other and might well learn and profit from that assistance.

► **Communicate Openly, and Publicly Test Assumptions and Beliefs**

Insist on being honest and on testing assumptions, even in difficult situations. For example, if Anne suspects Harry of starting a rumor about her, she can initiate a hallway conversation with him by asking a question like this: "Harry, someone started a rumor about me and Steve. What do you know about that story and how it got started?" Such directness may seem startling and dangerous to many managers, but Anne has little to lose and much to gain. Even if she does not get the truth from Harry, she lets him know that she is suspicious of his game and is not afraid to confront him.

► **Combine Advocacy with Inquiry**

Advocacy is expressed by statements that communicate what an individual thinks, knows, wants or feels. Inquiry involves behavior with the goal of learning what others think, know, want or feel. Here is a model of the relationship between advocacy and inquiry:

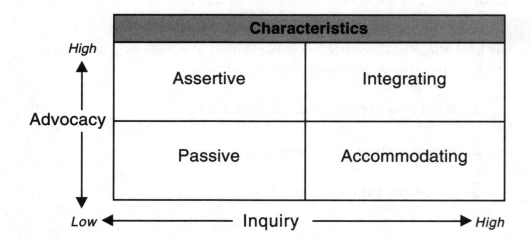

Characteristics	
Assertive	Integrating
Passive	Accommodating

High ↑ Advocacy ↓

Low ← Inquiry → High

In the previous situation, Anne might initiate a meeting with Harry to discuss the situation. To combine advocacy and inquiry, she would tell Harry what she thinks and feels while testing her assumptions and trying to learn from Harry. This is not an easy prescription; it is difficult to learn and practice. Such openness carries risks, and it's hard to be effective when you are ambivalent, uncomfortable or frightened. Try to be reasonably confident that you can cope with others' responses. Anne is likely to be comfortable confronting Harry only if she believes her skills permit her to cope with interpersonal challenge. On the other hand, if she tells herself that she doesn't deal well with people who are demanding, critical, angry or manipulative, she probably won't.

Building long-term cooperative relationships among co-workers is a long-standing challenge to many people. It's not easy—even when people try very hard to work together across various organizational and interpersonal conditions. In many situations, we need to do more than "try harder to get along." We also need to recognize inherent organizational barriers and address them.

EXERCISE: Reflection on Workplace Relationships

Complete the following evaluation.

1. I feel the need to compete with my peers.

1	2	3	4	5	6	7	8	9	10
low				medium					high

2. There is pressure from supervisors to compete rather than cooperate.

1	2	3	4	5	6	7	8	9	10
low				medium					high

3. I am uncomfortable speaking to others directly about a concern.

1	2	3	4	5	6	7	8	9	10
low				medium					high

4. My skills are not sufficient to allow me to cope with interpersonal challenges.

1	2	3	4	5	6	7	8	9	10
low				medium					high

5. People I work with are unaware that there are barriers to "getting along."

1	2	3	4	5	6	7	8	9	10
low				medium					high

Ideally, your answers should be in the low to medium range. Any answers marked above 5 indicate that there is work to be done to enhance workplace intercommunication and attitudes. One way this integration can be understood is through the concepts of *celebrity* and *reputation*.

BUILDING BETTER PEER RELATIONS

Abraham Maslow and many others have written that some human needs are common to us all. Two of the most influential needs in work relationships are the need to succeed and the need to be accepted by others. A major problem with peer relationships occurs because these two needs frequently conflict. It's tough to work well with people when you are competing with them for money, advancement and/or recognition—three things that most of us work for most of the time. Furthermore, we know that competition makes peers hypercritical of one another—hardly a quality that promotes acceptance. "I will help my coworker do better" is incompatible with "I need to do better than my coworker." The latter goal tends to triumph, and cooperative relationships are lost.

Because we know that peer competition can actually impede our work, as well as interfere with our need to be accepted, it is clearly not in our best interest to continue competing with our coworkers. Yet if we don't compete, how do we get our due respect? Peers need to learn how to integrate these two needs—the need to succeed and the need to be accepted—in a way that leads to successful behavior for all involved.

Celebrity

All of us are acquainted with celebrity: the big prizes that organizational contestants vie for to show that they did something special and get recognition from the organization. When celebrity is managed carefully, it can contribute to a person's long-term positive image and overall benefit. Most people, and almost all peers, compete for celebrity to some degree, as a means for moving up the organization.

Our organization rewards us by

_____

_____

Is the competition for celebrity friendly or has the competition become hostile?

_____

_____

BUILDING BETTER PEER RELATIONS
(continued)

Reputations

But there is another route to success in organizations, especially in peer relations, and that is by creating a reputation. Reputation is acquired gradually and is more enduring than celebrity status. We gain a positive reputation from being trustworthy, skilled at making things happen, and able to achieve goals through working well with people. Seeking our opinion, inviting our participation in a significant meeting, trusting us with confidential information, thanking us for the role played behind the scenes—all these are ways that people tell us we have built a credible, valuable reputation.

People who are effective in working with and through their peers tend to focus on building long-term reputation rather than short-term celebrity. Their strategy is to help their coworkers achieve celebrity—to give them credit, to let them be recognized, to help them stand out in the organization. When you give celebrity to your peers, you are helping them satisfy much of their need for recognition and acceptance. Most importantly, by assisting and encouraging your peers, you have also enhanced your own career, increasing your reputation. Your contribution is both valued and valuable, and you, too, achieve greater success. In essence, you satisfy your needs by helping your peers do the same.

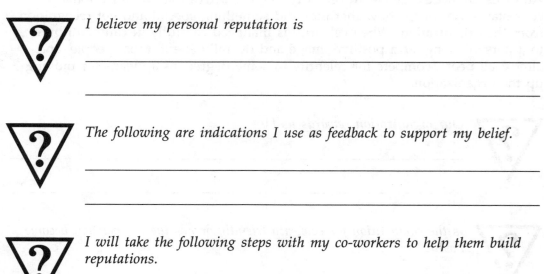

I believe my personal reputation is

_____

_____

The following are indications I use as feedback to support my belief.

_____

_____

I will take the following steps with my co-workers to help them build reputations.

_____

_____

BUILDING EMPATHY: TAKING OTHERS' NEEDS INTO CONSIDERATION

Another way to build healthy peer relationships is to recognize that coworkers are not fixed entities who have to be "dealt with" on an everyday basis, but rather are people—like us—who have ordinary feelings, thoughts, and varying ways of responding to their environment. It's important not to forget, as we interact with these individuals every day, that what we put out affects what we get back. Otherwise, we mistakenly think that the " bad" relationships we have with our peers come with the territory. Of course we can't simply make our coworkers disappear, so we may start to scheme about how to avoid them, be one up on them, or simply tolerate them. But we can begin to change the quality of our peer relationships from antagonistically cooperative to genuinely cooperative, by building into our daily interactions the interpersonal factors that bring people in working relationships closer together.

One crucial factor is empathy. Most people think of empathy as the ability to feel what someone else is feeling, to experience the work through another's eyes. In peer relationships, the term takes on a more subjective meaning: When we are empathetic, we exercise a mental flexibility that enables us to willingly consider the views of another while suspending our own judgment. When caught up in a discussion or a project, this *subjective empathy* helps us to see our coworker's point of view. We can achieve compromises and design new solutions that integrate our peer's work and move him or her in the same direction we are heading. Being empathic enables us to find the *common ground*.

In the next segment, we'll examine specific ways of achieving this common ground, through networking and consulting.

DEVELOPING COMMON GROUND

By identifying and solving problems, work gets done in organizations. Unfortunately, most problems don't come packaged and labeled like canned goods at a grocery store. It's not until someone identifies a situation as a problem that it becomes the focus of attention or the target for resources. Though some problems may be obvious, most are not.

 How do problems get noticed where you work?

_____

_____

Often you, or a peer, has a particular background or speciality (such as engineering, accounting or Human Resources) and will see an opportunity to improve work flow, minimize errors, or add value to a process. Maybe, however, the specialist doesn't have access to decision makers who are responsible for the process, or doesn't know how to influence those people. In such situations, it's not very helpful to just urge the specialist to take more initiative. Without a network of resources, and some skills and know-how in consulting across internal organizational boundaries, not much will happen.

Networking

A *personal network* is a group of people inside and outside the work group who are all "tuned to the same channel." These people share common values, goals, and aspirations, and the support they give to one another is invaluable. Here are some ways to build a network and tap into its benefits.

► **Work with Projects and People Who Are Highly Visible**

Make the effort to become friends. Propose a joint activity that will benefit both of you. If that goes well, you gain more recognition.

► **Create and Develop Informal Groups**

Some groups can support members who'd be weaker by themselves. Other informal alliances can influence goal and policy decisions and gain more control over resources. Informal groups can be powerfully good or powerfully destructive. Focus on doing what's best for the company in all alliances.

► **Be Alert for the Need to Form a Coalition**

Arrange frequent, informal get-togethers with your counterparts in other units or departments. Listen carefully for tidbits or news you can piece together later. Be acutely aware of unspoken signals between people. Take every opportunity to pursue common objectives. Talk to others informally at meetings, coffee breaks, waiting for the elevator. During a controversy, automatically and calmly guide the group. They'll turn to you for guidance in a crisis, and this can increase your influence.

Consulting

Positive peer interaction is rooted in collaborative relationships. Flexibility is basic to the kind of interdependence that allows people to openly share ideas, thoughts, and commitments.

The ability of a group to mesh personalities or styles—one person supply another's missing or underdeveloped traits—is what promotes long-term collaborative efforts. The two phrases, "Birds of a feather flock together" and "Opposites attract" seem contradictory on the surface but can be reconciled by focusing on the twin dynamics of *process* and *task.*

PROCESS: How things get done: The way people relate to each other, work-flow arrangements, etc.

TASK: What gets done: specific assignments, products produced, jobs, recommendations, etc.

In peer relations, the "birds of a feather" aspect has to do with the process: setting the climate, ground rules, or stage for our interactions. "Opposites attracting" has more to do with task orientation when we are relating to others.

It is important for all parties to be clear about both process and task issues in enhancing collaborative relationships across work group and organizational boundaries.

AVOIDING ACTIONS THAT IRRITATE YOUR PEERS

Problems that occur between people who work together on interteam and intergoup projects are rarely the result of true "personality conflicts." What may seem an intrinsic difference between people in many cases stems from other causes. Identifying the root cause can be difficult; following are some examples as well as some tips for avoiding them.

Being Out of Sync

People sometimes operate on different time systems. One result of this disparity is that the various parties have different definitions of "short-term" and "long-term." A work group may be operating in a high-action, high-stress environment. So to this group, short-term will mean in the next few days or weeks; long-term will be a few months ahead. Others, on the other hand, might think of long-term planning as stretching years into the future. This difference can lead to conflicts in which people feel pushed to allot time, energy and attention to distant issues, with no perceived relevance or payoff.

Another example of the disparity between two people from different work areas is a recurring difficulty in scheduling meetings. Sometimes one group expects their peers to be able to schedule a meeting on one or two days' notice, but these peers may be operating within tight personal schedules that cannot accommodate that need. Occasionally the reverse occurs. In both cases, however, the person with the narrower planning horizon may feel that the other lacks commitment and/or is avoiding the project. In fact, the underlying cause is simply structural: Out-of-sync time schedules will always be a stumbling block unless the parties can figure out a way to compromise.

Think back to a recent scheduling problem.

How did you end up resolving the time conflict?

_____

_____

_____

How did the parties end up deciding on a mutually agreeable time?
Were the people or groups aware of the problem of being out of sync,
or were the parties assuming other motives or causes to the scheduling
problem?

_____

_____

_____

Assuming Inappropriate Authority

Some of the worst conflicts on peer relationships have been caused by one person's attempt as assume inappropriate authority. Even if the peer is acknowledged as an expert, that person's attempt to teach by issuing orders and instructions is likely to cause resentment. The employee is still ultimately responsible for his or her own job performance and will resent the "experts" making decisions that will have to be defended. And the more the expert expects the peer to show obedience or deference, the wider this gap becomes, until the peer rejects even ideas and programs that are clearly beneficial. Ways will be found to quickly "remove" the bothersome staff person. If the expert attempts to control by using another executive's authority, this will also be unsuccessful. The specialist may gain initial compliance, but in the end the peer will still find a way to get free of the power game.

AVOIDING ACTIONS THAT IRRITATE YOUR PEERS (continued)

Being Arrogant

Don't make the error of placing a very high value on your own knowledge, ideas and opinions while dismissing your peer's ideas. You may have a great deal of experience, but using your expertise as a weapon is short-sighted and ill-timed. Like the result of incorrectly assuming decision-making authority, a condescending attitude will stimulate your peer to look for ways of rejecting what you do or suggest, out of simple resentment.

Another, more subtle form of arrogance occurs when the "expert" has been called in by a high-level executive. Employees who are below that executive's level in the hierarchy will resent any special relationship the expert has with the boss. Avoid making comments about inside information you may have, which your peers may not have access to. Even unintentional references to confidential information tends to generate fantasies about what's going on, why the expert is "really" there, and what surprise moves the boss is about to make. Secrecy can also solidify resentment against the expert, making his or her job at hand more difficult.

In general, arrogance toward your peer's views is both costly to your reputation and counterproductive to the task you need to get done. One way to protect yourself from the pull toward arrogance is to arrange for a third party to occasionally observe and critique your attitude and posture toward the client.

Deferring Too Much to Your Peers

Don't put so much weight on your peer's opinions that you defer even when you should not. Beware of failing to raise issues that contradict his or her beliefs. It's a mistake not to confront them even when you observe a poor approach to a problem. Don't avoid talking about differences; and take care to make propositions and suggestions that can be tested or evaluated. If you fall into the trap of overdeference, your peers may be frustrated by this, especially when they sense you have a lot more to offer. Rather than giving him or her a secure feeling about your expertise, you create a vague sense of uneasiness.

A third-party impartial observer, as well, may encourage this confusion on the peer's part. Be careful that this does not happen.

Remaining Too Abstract

A typical instance of nonsynchronization with others is expressing yourself in the abstract when the peer is trying to absorb tangible suggestions, guidance or products.

There are, fortunately, concrete methods that help to synchronize this situation.

- Make specific recommendations for action.

- Do a progress report that is free of technical jargon or a "problems and issues" paper that uses specific, everyday examples from your peer's own experiences.

- Write a thought piece that generalizes problems but also suggests new ways of looking at these problems.

- Conduct a workshop to plan a specific response to a certain problem.

The point is that if you do something that your peer can react to (regardless of how), you are more likely to meet their need for involvement and progress. Reports and papers, if done well, become indispensable tools that can be used by others even months later. These documents obviously serve the need for tangible "things" with which to work. An example: a set of proposed guidelines for effective team meetings, which provided a set of specific dimensions for members to use in testing their own group's effectiveness or proposing alternative guidelines.

Don't keep your peers in the dark while you are working your "magic." By keeping them in the picture and explaining things in simple terms, you help them understand *how* you produced what you did.

WHAT TO WATCH OUT FOR

Unless they are recognized and managed, certain aspects of the typical work situation can block the effectiveness of your contributions. Check any that you recognize that you have done.

- ☐ Giving help that is clearly unwanted, or giving it in such a way that you can't find out whether it is or isn't wanted

- ☐ Conceding to the role-shaping forces around you, instead of managing your own fate

- ☐ Focusing too much on single events and not paying attention to influencing patterns

- ☐ Accepting the measurement and evaluation of others (professional or nonprofessional) without any attempt to influence them and their standards

- ☐ Developing a kind of arrogance toward others; no longer respecting, listening to, learning, or adapting to their needs and environment

- ☐ Becoming dependent on the technical logic of your efforts and ignoring the process by which changes can actually be implemented

- ☐ Starting a project by masking unstated assumptions, thereby building in problems

OTHER CONSIDERATIONS

1. Role expectations are never explicit. If the demands on your contribution do not feel right, or if your peer is behaving differently than you would like, then it's worth investigating and attempting to renegotiate everyone's expectations.

Define these expectations as part of "business as usual," rather than as a crisis. Negotiation and renegotiation should feel like the natural and effective thing to do and not be interpreted as an automatic indication of failure. This attitude—nobody's perfect and we will change as soon as we recognize the need—is probably the most important one to establish. That's because it influences what you will disclose to one another and whether you will be able to see patterns rather than just your own piece of the action.

2. There is no one "right" role. Effective role definition depends on needs and resources. Part of your basic task is to help make conscious choices about the kinds of help needed. These roles may shift from one to the other over the course of a project. For instance, an information systems specialist may start in the expert mode, doing a specific project for a peer, and then shift to a process focus to develop the peer's familiarity with on-line terminal use and self-programming methods. With development of the peer's capacities, the specialist can then serve as a periodic resource advisor, at his or her peer's initiative. This is much more effective than being stuck in the expert mode, keeping the peer dependent and a constant energy drain. This kind of evolution works best if it is openly discussed and managed by everyone involved. If it is left to chance, there is no real test of whether the process is on track.

3. It is particularly useful to develop a common language in discussions with your peers. It's worth a good bit of effort to develop this common language, so that issues, problems, or changes in direction can be discussed and handled directly. Each of you may feel that your problems are caused by the other, rather than (as is often the case) being the result of something awry in role definitions or the structure of the helping process.

OTHER CONSIDERATIONS (continued)

4. A key usefulness is in creating structures (regular meetings, reports, informal discussions, rating sheets, or reports) that help you gather information about your own impact and effect. One of the few truths in human behavior is that the *consequences* of our actions don't necessarily match our *intentions*. We learn by creating structures through which we are informed regularly about the effects of our work. To receive this kind of information on a regular basis, we need to make it as easy as possible for clients to gather and present it. The easiest way to get feedback is to let it be known that you are open to evaluation of the effects of your product and process. This feedback process, plus built-in evaluation or checkpoints, encourage negotiation of roles when something isn't right. Consider these critiques normal business, not a crisis.

After reading all these considerations about how to perform in the internal advisory role, a basic question remains for you to answer: Are you in the right business?

What is personally satisfying to you? What facets of support work drive you crazy? What feels like growth and learning?

_____

_____

Which elements do you get from this kind of organizational role?

_____

_____

What would you be doing with your energy and expertise if you were not in an internal helping position?

_____

_____

P A R T

III

Making Peer Relationships Successful

MAKING PEER RELATIONSHIPS UNCONDITIONALLY CONSTRUCTIVE

A doctor measures the physical health of an individual by checking a few basic elements, such as the blood system, the nervous system, and the digestive system. To measure the health of a peer relationship, we need to look at the basic qualities that allow it to cope successfully with differences. There are six such qualities. When they are maintained in a peer relationship, that relationship is as constructive as it can be.

1. Balance Emotion with Reason

Many aspects of a relationship are not rational. We often react emotionally, not logically, in pursuit of some purpose. Emotions such as fear, anger, frustration and even love may influence otherwise thoughtful actions. Emotions are normal, necessary and often essential to problem solving. Wisdom is seldom found without them. Our emotions convey important information, help us gather our resources and inspire us to action. But when two people are trying to reconcile their differences, reason and emotion need to be in some kind of balance.

Certainly we cannot work well with another person when emotions overwhelm our reason. It's hard to make a wise decision in the middle of a temper tantrum! But logic alone isn't enough, either, for solving problems and building a peer relationship. If we can develop both reason informed by emotion, and emotion guided and tempered by reason, the balance we achieve is *working rationality*.

2. Work Toward Mutual Understanding

If we are going to achieve an outcome satisfactory to both parties and leave everyone feeling fairly treated, we need to understand each other's interests, perceptions, and notions of fairness. Unless *I* have a good idea of what *you* think the problem is, what you want and why, and what you think is fair, I won't be able to suggest an outcome that will meet both our interests. *You* will be handicapped unless you understand how *I* see things. Whether we agree or not, the better we understand each other, the better our chance of creating a solution we can both accept.

MAKING PEER RELATIONSHIPS UNCONDITIONALLY CONSTRUCTIVE (continued)

3. Building Good Communication

Understanding requires effective communication. Even though in general we may understand each other, the quality of a particular outcome and the efficiency with which it is reached are likely to depend on communication about that particular issue. To reach a compromise, we have to be able to communicate about our differences. With good communication, we get more than improved understanding; we also reduce suspicion. Believing that the other side has heard and understood our views, and we theirs, increases our chances of reaching a fair and balanced agreement. Within reasonable limits, improved communication means a better working relationship.

4. Be Reliable

My communication with you is not worth much if you do not believe me. A commitment that is made lightly or disregarded easily is often worse than no commitment at all. Certainly, blind trust is not the answer, since misplaced trust will damage a relationship more than healthy skepticism. But well-founded trust, based on honest and reliable conduct over a period of time, greatly enhances peers' ability to cope with conflict.

5. Use Persuasion Rather Than Coercion

In a particular transaction, peers may be more interested in the immediate outcome than in the long-term relationship. Each will try to affect the other's decisions, so the way this bargaining proceeds will have a profound effect on the quality of the relationship. On one hand, I can try to inspire your voluntary cooperation through education, logical argument, moral persuasion, and my own example. At the other extreme, I can try to coerce you by limiting your alternatives and by issuing warnings, threats, even extortion and physical force. The more coercive the influence, the less likely a fair outcome that seems legitimate to everyone involved. Among peers, persuasion rather than coercion will build a healthier relationship.

6. Learn Mutual Acceptance

To deal well with their differences, peers need to accept one another's worth. Feeling accepted and valued is a basic human psychological need. Unless you listen to my views, accept my right to have views that differ from yours, and take my interests into account, I am unlikely to want to work with you to resolve our differences. In addition, acceptance is a matter of degree, not an either/or phenomenon. Indeed, as peers' acceptance of one another increases, so does their ability to solve their problems wisely and effectively.

BE UNCONDITIONALLY CONSTRUCTIVE

When you are unconditionally constructive, you ensure that even if others reject your specific advice, the process will allow you and your peers to remain connected. This approach is summarized in the following chart, which incorporates the six qualities discussed in this section.

Unconditionally Constructive Attitudes	Why It's Good for the Relationship	Why It's Good for Me
1. Balance emotion with reason.	An irrational battle is less likely to be resolved.	I make fewer mistakes.
2. Work toward mutual understanding.	The better I understand you, the fewer collisions we will have.	The less I shoot in the dark, the better solutions I can invent and the better able I am to influence you.
3. Build good communication.	We both participate in making decisions. Better communication improves our decisions.	I reduce the risk of making a mistake, without giving up the ability to decide.
4. Be reliable.	It builds trust and confidence.	My words will have more impact.
5. Use persuasion rather than coerce.	When people are persuaded rather than coerced, both the outcome and the compliance are better.	By being open, I keep learning; it is easier to resist coercion if one is open to persuasion.
6. Learn mutual acceptance.	To deal well with our differences, I have to work with you and have an open mind.	By working with you and with reality, I remove obstacles to learn the facts and to persuading you on the merits of my position.

RESOLVING DIFFERENCES AMONG PEERS

Misunderstandings nearly always contribute to ongoing unsolved problems among peers. Indeed, the phrases "we have a misunderstanding" and "we have a problem" have become nearly synonymous. When a marriage or friendship falls apart, the partners often say, "We didn't understand each other anymore" or "We didn't see things the same way."

In some cases, our interpretation of a situation creates a problem in our heads that is not there in reality. Steve recently recalled how badly he felt about misunderstanding his three-year-old son. The boy had been picking at his dinner and getting down from his chair to play with his toys. Steve, reading the paper in another room, told his son to sit back down and eat. A minute later, the child walked out of the kitchen and came up to his father. Steve looked into the kitchen, saw food still on the plate, spanked the child, and sent him back into the kitchen. What Steve didn't know was that the boy had put a large bite of food into his mouth and was coming to show his father how much he was eating.

If peer relationships stumble because of a lack of understanding, it helps to examine the barriers to better understanding and ways to overcome those barriers. Misunderstandings arise for many reasons: I misspoke, you misheard; I had old data while you had the latest information; and so on. To the extent that these are problems of communication, the following suggests ways to ensure that peer communications are clear and effective.

Here are some barriers to understanding that each of us can resolve:

- We may not realize how little we understand.

- We may fear learning that we are "wrong."

- We may not know how to develop better understanding.

Remedies to these barriers can be pursued unconditionally, whether or not others agree to do so.

START BY ASKING, "WHAT DO THEY CARE ABOUT?"

Even when we are aware of our ignorance and open to new ideas, the problem of trying to understand others may be overwhelming. Often we do not understand even our closest friends. If we had to understand everything about everyone with whom we have a relationship, we wouldn't have time for much else.

Part of our reluctance to work toward understanding another person may come from a hesitancy to start a process without limits. You can soften this reluctance by limiting your attention to what is most important to solving problems. Ask: What are your interests in this situation? What are your perceptions of your peers and the problem at hand? What underlying values of yours may be at stake?

Define Interests

A good solution to a particular problem should meet your interest as well as your peers'. You can start improving your understanding of your peers, both in general and for the purpose of compromise, by exploring your own interests and those of others. When you understand the relevant interests— concerns, needs, wants, hopes and fears—the better chance you have of being able to satisfy them, at least minimally.

Define Perceptions

When two people look at a problem, they rarely see it the same way. Try to understand the viewpoint and perception of your peers. This improves your chances of resolving the problem successfully.

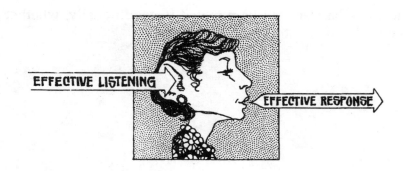

Take the Chance to Learn Something New

When you are trying to build a better relationship with someone you already know—particularly someone with whom you have a confrontational relationship—achieving understanding may mean unlearning some of your own preconceptions. Labor Relations personnel for a company with a history of union strikes, for example, will have some impression of the union leadership. Though this impression is no doubt partially valid, better understanding of the union leaders will probably mean the Labor Relations workers must abandon some of the old perceptions.

Unlearning can be uncomfortable. As you change your views, you will have to question some of your past decisions. You may fear that others will question your wisdom. This process is especially difficult when it touches on ideas you hold strongly. Because you are emotionally committed to these beliefs, you tend to avoid or ignore information that would contradict them. Sometimes our reluctance to listen and learn stems from fear: If we did learn more, for instance, we might discover that we had made mistakes in the past.

Be Open and Confident

One way to reduce the risk of being proven wrong is to avoid early commitments and remain open to new information. A union leader who says "We will consider every opportunity to avoid a strike, and we are always open to new ideas from management" will have an advantage. That leader will have more flexibility to negotiate good agreements and take advantage of management concessions than one who says (or implies), "We have decided to strike, and nothing you can say will change our minds."

Sometimes, it helps to take an initial position that communicates our intent, but leaves us open to other possibilities. Consider this example of a parent giving concession to a teenager:

"No, Terry, even though you feel broke, and even though your college expenses are higher than you expected, your mother and I have decided not to increase your monthly allowance, at least for now. If you will keep records for one month on where your money goes, and bring us a budget for the balance of the college year, we are prepared to consider an increase. We want a reasonable estimate of your needs, not one based on what you want or what the Millers are giving Jonathan."

START BY ASKING, "WHAT DO THEY CARE ABOUT?" (continued)

By maintaining confidence while remaining open, we can rule out unsatisfactory options without closing off all discussion. And in the light of new information, we can find new solutions and new views without any loss of face.

Learn Their Story

Think of the current situation or problem as the result of two stories—yours and your peers'. You know your story, but probably do not know theirs. What has happened to your peers? How did they get here?

A "story" should cover the events that brought another person into a relationship with you. And it should include a "plot"—the connections that brought these events together. A story may be the account of someone's life, or simply what happened to that person today that led up to an accident.

Learning someone else's story helps you overcome self-centeredness. It reveals facts, perceptions, and values that you would otherwise miss. Also, the better you know someone's story, the more likely that person is to become someone of value and concern to you. That concern will itself help you and your peers to work through your problems.

Reverse Roles

Try to imagine the other person's situation and assume their role. It helps to be as explicit as possible. If you are trying to understand your boss, you should imagine how it feels to sit in her office on the 34th floor; to meet with the regular Monday management committee, where her boss, the company president, grills her about the performance of her division; to be 56 years old with little chance to advance to the top spot; to have three children in college; and so forth.

With practice, we can use role reversal to more easily understand contrary points of view. Foreign service officers enhance their ability to understand other governments by altering the way they read news accounts or diplomatic reports. They can imagine themselves as the outlander who wrote the speech or delivered it, or as the person described in the dispatch, asking themselves: "How would I have to think and feel in order to be comfortable doing or saying those things without remorse? What end would justify those means in my estimation?"

The chance of our coming to understand our peers is far greater if we assume that others see themselves favorably, though we might not consider them so.

Draft a Charter of Their Choice

When we want to understand our peers' interests, perceptions, and values, we may not be clear about how to start or about what's important. It can help to focus on a specific choice *they* are facing.

In an ongoing relationship, there are likely to be some unresolved issues. Develop a charter that gives insight into how your associate may think about an issue. That lets you consider the choice your associate is facing, as seen by them. Then list the consequences—again, as seen by your associate—of your own decision. Your objective is a charter that will illuminate your associate's interests, values, and important perceptions. Think about the concerns of others, and imagine what choice you would make in those circumstances.

SUMMARY

The structure of many organizations today is vastly different from the highly centralized bureaucracies of the past. One revolutionary change has been the recent transformation toward more decentralized, collaborative organizations. Today's organizations attempt to create a high-performance, high-commitment culture through structural changes, changes in management style and the reorganization of work. Much has been written about the importance of such things as the physical layout of the workplace, selection and training practices for employees, the design of jobs, the formation of work teams, alternative pay practices and other human resource functions. All these elements take on new meaning in a collaborative environment.

Accompanying the shift to the more collaborative organization is the increased importance of lateral—peer—relationships for getting things done. These lateral relations demand new strategies for meeting goals and for effective performance. Successful people understand the nature of peer relationships and work to develop alternatives to the traditional hierarchical authority as a power base for exerting influence.

REFERENCES

Blake, Robert R. and Jane Mouton. *Consultation.* Reading, MA: Addison-Wesley, 1975.

Covey, Stephen R. *Seven Habits of Highly Effective People.* NY: Simon and Schuster, 1984.

Fisher, Roger and William Ury. *Getting to Yes.* NY: Penguin Books, 1988.

Hall, Douglas T. *Careers in Organizations.* Pacific Palisades, CA: Goodyear Publishing Co., 1976.

Katz, Elihu and Paul F. Lazersfeld. *Personal Influence.* NY: The Free Press, 1966.

McCall, Morgan. *The Lessons of Experience.* Lexington, MA: Lexington Books, 1988.

Maslow, Abraham. *Motivation and Personality.* NY: Harper and Row, 1954.

Peters, Thomas. *Thriving on Chaos.* NY: Knopf, 1987.

Schein, Edgar H. *Process Consultation.* Reading, MA: Addison-Wesley, 1969.

Sayles, Leonard. *Leadership: What Effective Managers Really Do.* NY: McGraw-Hill, 1982.

Steele, Fritz. *Consulting for Organizational Change.* Amherst, MA: University of Massachusetts Press, 1975.

Assessment

IMPROVING PEER RELATIONSHIPS

IMPROVING PEER RELATIONSHIPS

A FIFTY-MINUTE™ BOOK

The objectives of this book are:

1. to explain the need for attention to organizational peer relationships.

2. to discuss techniques of good peer relationships.

3. to point out problems in peer relationships.

OBJECTIVE ASSESSMENT FOR IMPROVING PEER RELATIONSHIPS

Select the best response.

1. In any organization, the information, resources and influence are passed
   A. from management to other employees.
   B. from side to side among peers.
   C. both of the above

2. Good communication should
   A. accompany action.
   B. precede action.
   C. follow action.
   D. all of the above

3. If some involved people are left out of communication that precedes action
   A. they can negatively affect the action.
   B. the action can proceed more quickly and effectively.

4. An opinion leader
   A. is someone in a position of authority.
   B. is usually acquainted with the attitudes of the group.
   C. usually makes judgements more quickly than others do.
   D. B and C
   E. all of the above

5. Those accepted as opinion leaders usually have
   A. superior attitudes.
   B. greater information.
   C. more prestige.

6. People band together
   A. to cope with stress.
   B. because they believe success will be most likely.
   C. for companionship.
   D. B and C
   E. all of the above

OBJECTIVE ASSESSMENT (continued)

Read this case study and then answer the questions that follow.

At ReFab, a synthetic fabric company, all marketing is through catalogs. Alison Kramer handles relations with catalog companies and quality control for fabric production. Larry McGuire, President, decides the company should hire a full-time marketing person to work with Alison and attend trade shows and relate to major customers. Larry interviews candidates along with Luke, the vice-president, and Tom, the controller. Georgianna is hired for the job and works many overtime hours to learn marketing processes; however, she holds the job only six months and then quits. Larry learns from Jess in the warehouse that Alison made life at ReFab unpleasant for Georgianna.

7. The most likely reason that Georgianna quit is that
   A. women in male-led companies often don't last.
   B. Alison's attitude made life at ReFab too unpleasant.
   C. she had to work overtime to learn marketing processes.

8. A mistake made by Larry was to
   A. hire Georgianna.
   B. allow her to work overtime.
   C. not invite Alison to the interviews.

9. The most likely reason Alison was unpleasant to Georgianna is that
   A. women don't work well with other women.
   B. she wanted the marketing job herself.
   C. she wasn't asked to participate in the job decision.

Select the best response.

10. In most middle- to large-sized companies, peer relationships
    A. involve competing interests.
    B. do not work well.
    C. are less frequent than in small companies.
    D. all of the above
    E. A and C

11. Relationships can most easily be quantified and defined in
    A. a hierarchical structure.
    B. a collaborative structure.

12. If employees interact frequently, they usually evolve easy methods of interfacing.
    A. True
    B. False

13. Body language is most easily interpreted in people you know
    A. well.
    B. slightly.

14. *Low cost* is often the most important consideration for
    A. a marketing department.
    B. an engineering department.
    C. a manufacturing department.

15. There is often more ambiguity in peer relationships than in hierarchical relationships.
    A. True
    B. False

16. A specialist working with a non-specialist should
    A. be accepted as an authority.
    B. communicate in the language of the non-specialist.

17. As organizations move to team structures, employee roles become
    A. more clear.
    B. less clear.

18. In peer relationships, it makes sense to
    A. emphasize common goals.
    B. combine advocacy with inquiry.
    C. test assumptions indirectly.
    D. all of the above
    E. A and B

19. Roles and relationships should be clarified before a project is attempted.
    A. True
    B. False

20. What may appear to be personality conflicts in peer relationships may be one individual's
    A. lack of group contact.
    B. arrogance.
    C. inappropriate authority.
    D. all of the above

21. For a relationship to be healthy, a balance must exist between
    A. fear and anger.
    B. reasoning and problem solving.
    C. reason and emotion.

OBJECTIVE ASSESSMENT (continued)

22. In general, relationships can be damaged more by
    A. blind trust.
    B. healthy skepticism.

23. In trying to understand another person, the best approach is to
    A. accept that you cannot understand.
    B. focus on understanding a particular situation.
    C. realize that with time and effort, we can understand.

24. A reason people may fear learning is that it will uncover mistakes made in the past.
    A. True
    B. False

25. Sophisticated human relations skills are more necessary in
    A. hierarchical organizations.
    B. collaborative organizations.

Qualitative Objectives for *Improving Peer Relationships*

To explain the need for attention to organizational peer relationships

Questions 1, 2, 6, 10, 14, 25

To discuss techniques of good peer relationships

Questions 4, 5, 12, 13, 18, 19, 21, 23

To point out problems in peer relationships

Questions 3, 7, 8, 9, 11, 15, 16, 17, 20, 22, 24

ANSWER KEY

1. C	**10.** E	**18.** E
2. D	**11.** A	**19.** A
3. A	**12.** A	**20.** D
4. D	**13.** A	**21.** C
5. B	**14.** A	**22.** A
6. E	**15.** A	**23.** B
7. B	**16.** B	**24.** A
8. C	**17.** B	**25.** B
9. C		

NOW AVAILABLE FROM
CRISP PUBLICATIONS

Books • Videos • CD Roms • Computer-Based Training Products

Subject Areas Include:

Management

Human Resources

Communication Skills

Personal Development

Marketing/Sales

Organizational Development

Customer Service/Quality

Computer Skills

Small Business and Entrepreneurship

Adult Literacy and Learning

Life Planning and Retirement

CRISP WORLDWIDE DISTRIBUTION

English language books are distributed worldwide. Major international distributors include:

ASIA/PACIFIC

Australia/New Zealand: In Learning, PO Box 1051 Springwood QLD, Brisbane, Australia 4127
Telephone: 7-3841-1061, Facsimile: 7-3841-1580 ATTN: Messrs. Gordon

Singapore: Graham Brash (Pvt) Ltd. 32, Gul Drive, Singapore 2262
Telephone: 65-861-1336, Facsimile: 65-861-4815 ATTN: Mr. Campbell

CANADA

Reid Publishing, Ltd., Box 69559-109 Thomas Street, Oakville, Ontario Canada L6J 7R4.
Telephone: (905) 842-4428, Facsimile: (905) 842-9327 ATTN: Mr. Reid

Trade Book Stores: Raincoast Books, 8680 Cambie Street, Vancouver, British Columbia, Canada V6P 6M9.
Telephone: (604) 323–7100, Facsimile: 604-323-2600 ATTN: Ms. Laidley

EUROPEAN UNION

England: Flex Training, Ltd. 9-15 Hitchin Street, Baldock, Hertfordshire, SG7 6A, England
Telephone: 1-462-896000, Facsimile: 1-462-892417 ATTN: Mr. Willetts

INDIA

Multi-Media HRD, Pvt., Ltd., National House, Tulloch Road, Appolo Bunder, Bombay, India 400-039
Telephone: 91-22-204-2281, Facsimile: 91-22-283-6478 ATTN: Messrs. Aggarwal

MIDDLE EAST

United Arab Emirates: Al-Mutanabbi Bookshop, PO Box 71946, Abu Dhabi
Telephone: 971-2-321-519, Facsimile: 971-2-317-706 ATTN: Mr. Salabbai

SOUTH AMERICA

Mexico: Grupo Editorial Iberoamerica, Serapio Rendon #125, Col. San Rafael, 06470 Mexico, D.F.
Telephone: 525-705-0585, Facsimile: 525-535-2009 ATTN: Señor Grepe

SOUTH AFRICA

Alternative Books, Unit A3 Sanlam Micro Industrial Park, Hammer Avenue STRYDOM Park, Randburg, 2194 South Africa
Telephone: 2711 792 7730, Facsimile: 2711 792 7787 ATTN: Mr. de Haas